EIGHT KEYS TO LEADING OTHERS

DR. RON KENOLY

THE EFFECTIVE PRAISE & WORSHIP LEADER
by Ron Kenoly

Parsons Publishing House
P. O. Box 6428
Panama City, FL 32404 USA
www.ParsonsPublishingHouse.com
Info@ParsonsPublishingHouse.com

All Scripture quotations, unless otherwise indicated, are taken from the Holy Bible, King James Version, Cambridge, 1769.

Scripture quotations marked "NKJV™" are taken from the New King James Version®. Copyright © 1982 by Thomas Nelson, Inc. Used by permission. All rights reserved.

Scripture quotations marked "TEV" are taken from The Good News Bible: Today's English Version, New York: American Bible Society, ©1992. Used by permission. All rights reserved.

Cover Design by Diane Parsons and Steve Tyrrell of Tyrrell Creative Design, www.TyrrellCreativeDesign.com.

Printed in the United States of America.
For World-Wide Distribution.
Published by Parsons Publishing House.

International Standard Book Number:
13 digit: 978-1-60273-004-5
10 digit: 1-60273-004-0
Library of Congress Control Number: 2007936844.

My prayer is that we will all sanctify our lives, overcome our divisions, give without measure, develop and offer our skills for the glory of God and become one as worshipers of the Most High God.

FROM THE EDITOR:

In this book, we have chosen to establish gender neutrality in reference to the worship leader. We have done this by referring to the worship leader as "he"in many places. This was done to allow for ease of reading and continuity. We believe that God calls, anoints and uses women as worship pastors, worship directors, worship coordinators, choir directors, etc. It is our belief that God uses women in leadership and support roles throughout ministry areas.

TABLE OF CONTENTS

*A worship leader
is a facilitator of the
activities that go on in the
presence of God.*

PREFACE

Praise and worship begins in the heart of a believer and ascends directly to the throne of God. While the focus of this book is for people involved in music ministry, every member of the body of Christ is called to praise and worship. Every Christian will benefit from these timeless truths. Whether you are leading your family or the person next to you, everyone is called to be an effective praise and worship leader.

In main-stream Christendom, the role of the contemporary praise and worship leader has been generally undervalued and misunderstood. Pastors and other pulpit ministers depend on the worship leader to prepare an environment for the manifest presence of God. During the praise and worship portion of the service, church leaders want the hearts and minds of the congregation to be ready to receive the prepared word given from the pulpit.

Many times church leaders do not understand how to specifically accomplish that task. They do know that they want good anointed music; that is one of the things that many appointed worship leaders and pastors have in common.

Sometimes you have praise and worship leaders who do not understand what they are supposed to accomplish in the natural or spiritual realms. Yes, they may sing well or even be a gifted musician, but they do not really know how to facilitate the manifestation of the presence of God.

Far too many times, the music ministry in the local church is made up of unskilled volunteers who make themselves available to help and serve. Of course, we praise God for these wonderful servants of the Lord. So many give their time and energy to serve with loyalty and faithfulness. On the other hand, many of them have no training regarding the purpose of praise and worship. Their lack of knowledge can prohibit the local church body from attaining a praise and worship experience that is pleasing to God. It is up to the leader to share their knowledge and experience with their group.

God is holy and His presence must be respected and protected. Jesus said in John 4:24 that those who worship God must worship in spirit and truth. He has an expectation about the attitude you must embrace for your worship to be acceptable.

Worship in spirit and truth requires more than fancy vocal aerobics, beautiful poetic lyrics and sweet or hot musical passages on the instruments. God is pleased with our talents, but He is not impressed by them. We must remember that every good and perfect gift comes from the Father (James 1:17). Worship leaders must be prepared to properly demonstrate a balance between worship and the Word. Just knowing the music and sounding good is not all that God requires of true worshipers. God is always looking at the heart of the worshiper.

In this book, I want to share eight keys which are crucial to leading others. My prayer is that it will help the contemporary praise and worship leader transform their role into an effective praise and worship leader.

Expected Roles for a Worship Leader

- Chief musician
- Administrator
- Vocal leader
- Pastoral skills

ONE

WHAT ARE PASTORS LOOKING FOR?

What are pastors really looking for in a worship leader?

As I travel around the world, I am often asked by pastors to recommend someone who could lead worship for their congregation. When they ask me this question, I am often reluctant to give answers or recommendations right away. I try to get them to a private place where we can talk, and find out exactly what they are trying to accomplish in their church and their worship services.

Many times I begin the conversation by asking them, "What kind of person are you looking for?" Just knowing a pastor needs a praise and worship leader is not enough information to make a recommendation. A well-rounded worship leader is someone who can be competent in several areas of church ministry. Let's look at these various roles.

Chief musician

The worship leader must have vocal skills that are smooth and enjoyable and not offensive to the people he is trying to lead. A congregation could be offended by a voice that is too high, too low, too intimate or too brash. He must be able to communicate appropriately the language of music with other singers and musicians. A worship leader should be able to assign vocal and musical parts to people who are capable of performing with skill and excellence. This requires good delegation and assessment skills.

Good vocal leader

It is a must for the vocal leader to be able to sing on pitch and be able to establish a melody that the congregation can learn, follow, and appreciate. He must have a charismatic ability to exhort and encourage the people to actively participate in celebrating the God of our salvation. Because he is one of the first people the congregation will see in the service, he will be creating the first impression. Therefore, he must be dressed in a way that will not offend or distract the followers, or embarrass the leadership of the congregation. The worship leader should serve as a reflection of the church and the pastor.

Administrator

Administration is an integral part of the worship leader's job. The ideal candidate must be able to plan and coordinate schedules and rotations. Understanding and executing the vision and mandate of the pastoral leadership will be expected. It is absolutely critical that the worship leader is able to submit to the leadership of the church. This person must be able to attend to the many details that accompany leadership roles such as:

- Keeping records
- Acquiring necessary tools and materials
- Assigning and delegating responsibilities
- Executing disciplinary actions
- Managing finances
- Representing the department in staff meetings

Pastoral skills

The praise and worship leader must have a heart for the people in the music department and the church. This person must demonstrate a heart of love for the people who are subordinate to him. Many times this includes:

- Counseling
- Praying
- Visitations

- Writing letters of recommendation
- Bible teaching
- Demonstrating spiritual leadership

The people he leads should need know that he loves them and genuinely cares about their concerns for ministry and their personal lives.

A balanced and effective music department should always be accompanied by a balanced and effective leader. Just having good musical skills is not sufficient for leading one of the most varied groups of people in the church. It is possible that the works of the flesh such as pride, ego, selfishness and lust for power and control will overtake and destroy a music department if the leader is lacking in any of the previously mentioned areas.

In 1 Corinthians 14:40, we see that all things must be done decently and in order. God is glorified through order and design. Confusion, tension, timidity, chaos and frustration are not of God and should not be found in the church or the music department.

A worship leader is to demonstrate before the people what God wants in the form of praise and worship.

The Effective *P&W* Leader Must:

- Be a good Christian in good standing
- Be able to teach and train
- Have common sense and wisdom
- Have fundamental musical knowledge
- Demonstrate leadership skills
- Have good manners and social graces
- Be committed to the pastor's vision

TWO

KEY #1: LEADERSHIP

Be a Christian in good standing with his pastor and church leadership

A good worship leader is going to need the endorsement and support of the pastoral staff and leadership of the church. The continual presence of this person in front of the congregation will cause the people to see them as a respected leader of the church. He may not have any authority outside the music department; he may not have a key to the building or access to any monies or accounts of the church, but the people will look at him as an important leader in the congregation. Everyone will know his name and expect him to lead them into an awareness of the presence of God.

His character must be above reproach and he must exhibit love, compassion and sensitivity toward others. The pastor needs to be able to trust him in personal, practical and spiritual matters.

High moral character is a must. Many music departments are filled with people who are overly passionate and capable of being led astray by their admiration of people who possess unique talent or exercise command and authority. Lust, greed, pride and abuse of power are spirits that are always waiting for an opportunity to manifest and destroy the effectiveness of a music department.

Be able to teach and train

Leaders must be able to teach and train others. The leader must first have musical and ministerial training - even if it's on the job training. If your church does not have the budget to assist you in your training, become self-taught through books and online resources. As you pursue your own education, there are many conferences and workshops available for worship leaders.

Many of the people in the music department may have little or no musical training and it's up to you to train them correctly. Your volunteers will not necessarily know the language of music or have the ability to read the notations in songbooks or sheet music. Often it seems like some of the people with the best voices and passion for music have the least amount of musical skills. Many of these people are self taught and have developed habits that need to be unlearned in order to work effectively with the group.

Some people are more gifted as soloists and some are more gifted as choir members. I have encountered countless situations where a person might have great solo singing voice, but not have the training and sensitivity to sing in a choral group. By themselves they are good, but with a group they stand out like a sore thumb and make the group ineffective. With education and guidance, a good worship leader will help transition the soloist into a group. The discernment of the leader will help uncover the group members that may need to be exhorted to use their gift as a soloist. It is a great goal to expand and stretch your members. We should always encourage each other to greater levels of excellence. A living ministry will always grow. The leader should expect the group as a whole and the members, in particular, to go from glory to glory.

Just as any Christian, the worship leader should speak words that edify and minister grace. As they develop the art of spiritual diplomacy, the lead singer needs to train and encourage people to sing together without squelching their spirit or discouraging them. This skill does not utilize false flattery, but speaking the truth in love. Sometimes it may mean that you direct a person to another area of service. 1 Corinthians 12:17-18 says, "If the whole body were an eye, where were the hearing? If the whole were hearing, where were the smelling? But now hath God set the members every one of them in the body, as it hath pleased him." The Lord sets us where He would have us and He often uses our leadership to help direct us to the proper area.

It's important for the director to foster unity and a sense of camaraderie. All are working together for the common good to lift up their voices to the Lord. In Psalm 34:3 King David admonished the people to exalt the name of the Lord together. He wrote "Oh magnify the Lord with me. Let us exalt His name together." We must remember that it takes all of us working together to accomplish God's purpose. The Apostle Paul explained it this way, "From whom the whole body fitly joined together and compacted by that which every joint supplieth, according to the effectual working in the measure of every part" (Ephesians 4:16). The body will increase as we all effectively work together.

Have common sense and wisdom

Common sense is not as common as it used to be. There is an old proverb that says, "A handful of common sense is worth a bushel of learning." The leader needs to be able to think logically and process thoughts clearly. He needs to be able to translate ideas and resolve issues with diplomacy and integrity. It is important to create a simple system of operation that everyone in the music department can understand and easily follow.

This person needs to be able to plan and coordinate programs, services, song lists and personnel. Delegating jobs and responsibilities to others who are qualified to help in the music department are also important for this position.

Demonstrate leadership skills

Sometimes we may find that our faithfulness and godly character have elevated us to a place of leadership for which we do not feel qualified. Anyone can learn to be a leader. The director would do well to pursue personal education and training to develop leadership skills. No matter at what level you find yourself, educate yourself to become better – better at music – better at ministry – better at leadership.

The leader must be able to establish and maintain order and control of meetings and rehearsals. A take-charge attitude and command for respect of the appointed position brings security to your group. General George Patton described the most important quality of a good leader as one that is willing to make decisions. I'm not saying that he needs to be a tyrant, but the leader needs to hold the floor and control the flow of the meetings where he is in charge. The presence of the director should encourage people to give their undivided attention when he speaks. The buck stops with the leader being able to boldly diffuse rebellion and disrespectful confrontations immediately. Resolving conflicts between people in the music department and bringing them to an awareness of scriptural and godly behavior. Every conflict resolution needs to have a biblical reference.

The leader must be willing and able to give personal counsel to members of his group, according to his own ability and qualifications. It is important to impart pertinent wisdom and knowledge. Some churches may call this position the *worship pastor.* It is the senior pastor's decision whether there is an expectation for the worship leader to pastor and shepherd the flock in the music department under the authority of the senior pastor.

Success is when preparation meets opportunity. The leader must be punctual for each meeting, and be prepared to lead his group with confidence and authority. The success of any rehearsal or meeting will be determined by the preparation prior to the meeting. Leaders must lead by example, so the worship leader must be prepared to set the standard of godly behavior for the people who follow him.

When the leader is not respectful of meeting times--continually late or does not start on time--those who follow him will assume that tardiness is an acceptable behavior. Tardiness has never been, and will never be, acceptable behavior in the business of the church or in the house of the Lord. American playwright Don Marquis said, "Punctuality is one of the cardinal business virtues: always insist on it in your subordinates." Tardiness can destroy the effectiveness of a program. It can cause anger and resentment in the hearts of the people who make the effort to be where they ought to be at the appointed time. The leader should make a decision not to establish the foundation of ministry on low standards which lead to ineffectiveness.

Have fundamental musical knowledge

The leader must have fundamental musical knowledge. It is difficult to lead others in an arena of ministry in which you have no academic knowledge. There are those in the group you are leading who will expect to follow someone who has made the same investment of time and study to improve their skill. It will be hard for them to give their full respect to someone who has not taken that same initiative.

Executing music properly requires skill. The more people involved in ministry, the more training and education you need to deliver your ministry presentation with accuracy and effectiveness. You must be able to communicate your requirements and interpretation to others in correct musical terms. Learn to speak the language of music. If you do not know music theory, embark now on learning this discipline.

Without a fundamental knowledge of music, a leader will be limited when it comes to taking his group to higher levels in productions, orchestrations and arrangements. As believers we are called to bypass mediocrity and pursue excellence. Psalm 8:1 says, "O Lord our Lord, how excellent is thy name in all the earth!" Our God is excellent and we should continually strive to give Him a more excellent offering of worship and praise.

Display manners and etiquette

The leader is responsible for producing a congenial environment for people to feel loved, wanted and accepted. Saying "please" and "thank you" are always appreciated and are a great encouragement for getting people to work together. Supreme Court Justice Clarence Thomas noted, "Good manners will open doors that the best education cannot."

Most of the people who participate in the music department are volunteers. They make great personal sacrifices to serve in the church. The leader must let these people know that they are appreciated and needed. People take time away from their families and sometimes their jobs to donate their talents, skills and abilities to help the church advance in its outreach. They need to be reminded that what they are doing is wanted, needed and appreciated. Colossians 3:15 encourages all Christians to "be ye thankful." Choose to develop and express a thankful heart to God and those around you.

Be committed to the pastor's vision

The praise and worship leader must have a good understanding of the pastor's vision for the church and be submitted and committed to that vision. His own personal agenda must not be a threat to the pastor or the church's goals and objectives. There is only room for one vision in a church, anything else would be di-vision.

It is not unusual for a worship leader to feel that he has a better plan for the church service than the pastor. Many times the people in the music department feel they need more time for the song services. I've got news for you...most pastors feel they need more time to preach.

It is a natural thing for creative people to have ideas about how things should go. But on the other hand, the Holy Spirit has a plan also. The Spirit of God will reveal to the pastor His will for the services. Since the church belongs to the Lord, it is a good idea to let the Lord have His way. God's anointing begins with the pastor. Worship leaders need to be under their pastor's anointing and work with it.

> *Behold, how good and how pleasant it is for brethren to dwell together in unity! It [unity] is like the precious ointment [anointing] upon the head, that ran down upon the beard, even Aaron's beard: that went down to the skirts of his garments (Psalm 133:1-2).*

In this passage of Scripture, it is clear that unity and anointing are directly related. Anointing begins at the head and flows to the submitted parts of the body. Every body part that is submitted under the head will receive the same anointing as the head. God gives anointing according to the plans and purposes He has for an individual or a group.

Many times while my pastor, Dr. Dick Bernal, was preaching or teaching, the Holy Spirit would be giving me songs from the message that was being delivered. The rest of the congregation would be taking notes, but God would speak to my heart in the way of a song.

Be reminded of the lesson to be learned when Lucifer set his heart on overthrowing the will of God:

> *Thou art the anointed cherub that covereth; and I have set thee so: thou wast upon the holy mountain of God; thou hast walked up and down in the midst of the stones of fire. Thou wast perfect in thy ways from the day that thou wast created, till iniquity was found in thee. By the multitude of thy merchandise they have filled the midst of thee with violence, and thou hast sinned: therefore I will cast thee as profane out of the mountain of God: and I will destroy thee, O covering cherub, from the midst of the stones of fire. Thine heart was lifted up because of thy beauty, thou hast corrupted thy wisdom by reason of thy brightness: I will cast thee to the*

ground, I will lay thee before kings, that they may behold thee (Ezekiel 28:14-17).

Lucifer was cast down to the lowest depths of the pit. His personal lust and ambition cost him his position, his prestige and his title. It caused him to be utterly removed from the very presence of God. The consequences for getting God upset are more than any of us want to bear.

The Effective P&W Leader Must:

- Have a good knowledge of the Bible
- Know what your denomination or movement believes
- Know that the pastor is ultimately the worship leader
- Know that all of Christianity is about authority and submission

THREE

KEY #2: KNOWLEDGE

Have a good knowledge of the Bible

Many popular songs are not scriptural. There are several songs that traffic through the body of Christ that are not in compliance with the Scriptures. These songs may be played on the radio, television or on other popular media devices. The effective worship leader will review the lyrics of every song and make sure that he is not teaching something through music that is out of alignment with the Word of God.

Don't rely on the people who work in the record industry to make songs that are contextually accurate. We thank God for the contributions that the Christian music industry makes toward providing inspirational recordings for the body of

Christ; however, accuracy of Scripture is not always at the top of their agenda. Record companies are businesses that must make a profit in order to justify their existence. Therefore, these companies must present music to the religious public that will have popular catch phrases, easy hook lines, haunting rhythms and beautiful melodies that passionately drive the listeners to purchase the song that they can't get out of their minds.

Many of the decision makers in the record companies know music and trends of the industry, but have limited experience with the Bible and the doctrines of the church. Their music may sound good to the ear, but may be dangerous to the mind and the spirit. On numerous occasions I have been surprised by how many people there are making major decisions in the Christian music industry that are not even Christians or have a very weak, shallow walk with the Lord.

The worship leader should be a filter between the music industry and the local church congregation. They must protect their congregations by screening all of the material that is presented in their local church. Even the solos that people sing must be consistent with what is to be taught in the Bible and in your local body.

Know what your denomination or movement believes

Know what your denomination or your movement believes so that you can lead people with confidence. Confidence comes from knowing that the words to the songs are in line with the Word of God and your local congregation.

Your denomination may not agree with popular song texts. You must have a good understanding of what your denomination teaches or emphasizes. Churches and denominations have different types of services and every song that is scriptural may not be acceptable to certain groups.

On one particular occasion, I was invited to lead a praise and worship concert in a city in Washington State. Before each meeting, I like to meet with the pastor to pray and find out if there is anything in particular that he wants me to do or not do during the service.

In our pre-service meeting, this particular pastor explained to me that he was trying to love people into the Kingdom, as opposed to scaring them away from hell. He asked me if I would avoid singing any of my songs that mentioned hell or the devil.

Those of you who are familiar with my recordings know that I have many songs that mention satan, hell and the devil. I don't have a problem with singing songs about victory over the enemy; Jesus talked about hell and the devil on several occasions. However, if the pastor of a church feels that the mention of these things will frighten or confuse his congregation, I will respect his wishes and avoid singing any songs that will upset his policies and plans.

I can lead people in praise and worship without mentioning the devil. In my spirit I did not understand why this particular pastor felt that he had to be so passive and non-confrontational with the enemy. I must assume that the pastor always has a word from God and divine instructions from the Holy Spirit about how to conduct his services.

The pastor is ultimately the worship leader

The greatest role model for worship in a local body is the pastor. He is responsible before God for his congregation. I may only be invited there to help in the praise and worship services for a few days. As a worship leader, it is not my place to impose my personal ideas about how a pastor should run his church services. He is the ordained authority in that church; I have a responsibility, as his guest, to submit to his ordinances and procedures.

All of Christianity is about authority and submission

It is vitally important for worship leaders to know that their position is, and always will be, a subordinate position to the pastor. If you are considering a song that could create confusion or controversy, take it to the pastor and get his thoughts about the song. Don't embarrass your pastor by surprising him with song lyrics about which he may later have to apologize. Avoid having him come to you after the fact, and tell you not to sing a particular song again.

In September of 1985, I began as worship leader at Jubilee Christian Center in San Jose, California. This was my very first job on staff as a worship leader. I had been attending a traditional denominational Bible college in Marin County, California.

Jubilee Christian Center is by no means traditional or denominational. It is an independent, Word of Faith, spirit-filled, high energy, charismatic church that flows in the anointing of God and freely exercises all the gifts of the Holy Spirit.

There were several times Pastor Dick had to correct me in my choice of songs. Because of my traditional background, there were many songs that were not appropriate for the Jubilee congregation and the Word of Faith movement. Most of those forbidden songs were wonderful and celebrated in the former churches I had attended, but not at Jubilee. I had to really study what our movement embraced to make sure that every song I taught the congregation was consistent with what Pastor Dick was preaching from the pulpit.

A worship leader must spend time with the Father and find out what He wants us to do.

An Effective *P&W* Leader Must:

- Have a living testimony
- Minister with conviction and boldness
- Sing with passion and spirit
- Deliver ministry that comes from the heart

FOUR

KEY #3: TESTIMONY

Have a living testimony

It is essential to have a living testimony of what God has done in your life. Your experience with God will be reflected in your worship leading. Every worship leader should know the power of God. How can you sing songs about a God that you have not personally experienced? When you stand before people to lead them in worship, you need to know that the things you are singing about are real and relevant in your own life experiences. The songs should come from your heart and spirit, and not just from your head and mouth. Examine your life experiences; pinpoint the times when you prayed and believed God for a certain thing to happen and God answered your prayer. When you sing about that type of experience, it will come from deep within your spirit.

Minister with conviction and boldness

When you sing from your spirit, a song will come forth with conviction and boldness. When you know from your own personal experience that God is able to hear and answer our prayers, your confidence will be evident.

Sing with passion and spirit

When I was a little boy, I would hear my mother sing all the time. It didn't matter if she was in the church choir loft or standing over the kitchen sink. All of my mother's songs seemed to have passion and spirit. There were many obstacles in our lives during those years in our hometown of Coffeyville, Kansas. While my brothers and I were growing up, my mother had to lean heavily on her trust in God's ability to bring us from one day to the next. The songs that she sang always seemed to bring her strength and peace. When she sang the song "Great Is Thy Faithfulness," I believed that God was faithful just because of the confidence with which she sang that song. Over the years, I have chosen to lean toward songs to which I can attach my personal testimony. These songs come from deep within my soul. They testify of the Father's goodness, mercy and truth. Jesus encourages us to worship the Father in spirit and truth.

> *But the hour comes, and now is, when the true worshippers shall worship the Father in spirit and in truth: for the Fa-*

> *ther seeks such to worship him. God is a Spirit: and they that worship him must worship him in spirit and in truth (John 4:23-24).*

When we worship in spirit and truth, we have the assurance that the Holy Spirit is leading us. We cannot go wrong when we follow Him without distraction.

Ministry needs to come from your heart

Ministry should come from your heart and spirit, not just your mouth. God looks at our heart. He looks past our talents and outer appearances and focuses on the attitudes found there. If the song that you are singing is not in your heart, then it cannot be done in spirit or truth. A song that does not bear witness to your spirit is merely a showpiece. God is not interested in a show. He does not want to be entertained; He wants praise and worship to be holy, honest and true.

The Effective P&W Leader Must:

- Have a disciplined prayer life
- Pray about song selections
- Position oneself to receive anointing
- Be willing to lead others in prayer
- Encourage others in the Lord and the Word of God

FIVE

KEY #4: PRAYER

Have a disciplined prayer life

There is no substitute for a consistent and quality relationship with the Lord. You must learn how to pray without ceasing, as the Apostle Paul instructs us to do in 1 Thessalonians 5:17. It is through your relationship with God in prayer, that the Holy Spirit will give you instructions about how to lead your music department and how to make important decisions. The Bible says in Proverbs 3:6, "In all your ways acknowledge Him and He will direct your paths."

You need to start each day with a time of personal prayer and devotion. Many people make a prayer list so they can remember all of the things about which they need to pray. Others have a fixed list that they pray on a routine basis.

Some people pray spontaneously about whatever comes to their mind at the moment.

I have learned to pray all three ways. When people ask me to pray about specific things, I try to write them down so I will not forget. So many times nowadays my mind gets cluttered. I have a tendency to forget about things that others ask me to do if I don't keep some type of list.

In my early morning devotional, I have a routine prayer that I pray. It will include:

- Praise and worship
- Praying for forgiveness
- Praying for my immediate family and myself
- Praying for our World Vision® children, extended family and friends
- Praying for my ministry, staff, band and board of directors
- Praying for my businesses
- Praying for my pastor and our church congregation
- Praying for our local pastors and leaders
- Praying for our nation and our president
- Praying for the peace of Jerusalem
- Praying for the peace of Israel and other parts of the world
- Praying in the spirit
- A time of quietness and meditation so that I can hear Him speak to me

Sometimes I am amazed at how fast the time goes by. All through the day I am asking the

Lord to help and guide me in making right decisions. I know that I need the wisdom of God and we should not be hesitant about asking Him to show us His ways. Being a creative person, I have many ideas that pass through my brain each day. All of my ideas seem like good ideas, but what I need are God ideas. I only need to process thoughts that come from the heart and the will of the Father. We must allow the mind of Christ to be formed in us.

Disciplined prayer life

Every facet of ministry must be bathed in prayer. I pray about song selections for meetings for which I might be preparing. I pray about choosing the right meeting from the many invitations I receive. I pray about people I hire and how to lead the people that work for and with this ministry. I pray about future plans, goals and objectives. I pray over management strategies and other administrative matters. I PRAY ALL THE TIME!

You cannot lead others where you have not been. When you have spent time with God, it will show. Your confidence will increase because you will know that you have heard from God. You will become bold in all of your efforts. You will sense the presence of the Holy Spirit in your thoughts, deeds and actions. Jesus said in John 10:27, "My sheep know my voice." We must spend enough time with Him to know His voice beyond a shadow of a doubt.

No one wants to follow someone who is timid and uncertain. People will always tend to follow strong, confident leaders who know where they are going and what they are going to accomplish when they get there.

Position oneself to receive the anointing

When the worship leader has spent time with God, there will be an anointing that overshadows him. It is that anointing which empowers him to effectively lead the people of God into His presence. The anointed worship leader will know and understand the importance of creating an environment for the presence of God. He must follow as the Holy Spirit leads, without fear of people's opinions.

Those who truly want to worship in spirit and truth will recognize the anointing and enter into a pure attitude of worship toward the Father.

Be willing and able to lead others in prayer

As a leader, you will always need to build up and encourage the people who are subordinate to you. They will depend on you to help them solve their problems and issues. You are expected to have the answers and solutions to their problems which they can't solve. If you don't have the answers, they expect you to find the answers or pray a miracle into their lives. Sometimes they just need help to make it to the next day.

Encourage others in the Lord through the Word

That is exactly what you must do. You must be able to encourage your followers and show them what God has to say in the Bible about their problems. You will need to believe with them, in faith, for divine intervention in their situation. You must always help them know that God will not allow them to bear more than they can stand. Whoever calls on the name of the Lord will be saved and delivered.

You cannot afford to have a group of followers who don't believe what they are singing about in their songs. We sing about the greatness and the faithfulness of God and we must know about it on a personal level.

The Effective *P&W* Leader Must:

- Be bold in leading worship
- Be punctual
- Establish and maintain order
- Know your limitations
- Use your authority wisely
- Demonstrate love and respect
- Make eye contact with the people
- Be sensitive to your congregation
- Avoid tongue lashing
- Teach the people whenever possible

SIX

KEY #5: BOLDNESS

Be bold in leading worship

Establish authority and order in the service. When you stand before a congregation to lead them, you have been given a certain amount of authority. You must find out how much authority you have. You don't want to offend the church leadership by assuming duties or responsibilities that are not yours or extend over into another person's realm. Sometimes it just takes communication with your leadership for you to walk confidently in your position. Your duties should be carried out with boldness and confidence.

Be punctual

If it is your responsibility to begin the service, you must start the service on time. It may mean telling the people to settle down, stop talking and take their places so that corporate attention may be given to the Lord Jesus Christ. They will need to be taught what you expect of them.

You must start and stop on time. God is a God of order and design; He wants everything to be done in an orderly fashion. As it says in 1 Corinthians 14:40, "Let all things be done decently and in order."

God has eternity, but He has given us time to live by. In nature, He demonstrates how everything has its own season. Summer, autumn, winter, and spring all come at an appointed time as ordained by their Creator. If the seasons were changed, it would constitute a rebellion against God. The sun, moon, earth and stars are established on a certain course. If they should change their course, mankind would perish immediately.

Pastors pray about the order of service and its content. When they establish a certain time for a particular activity, they are following a pattern set by the Holy Spirit for their local body. When, and if, we disregard those timetables, we are in direct rebellion against the Holy Spirit. We do not have the right to change a mandate that God has given to the pastor or the service organizers.

That may sound strong, but it is true. When we start service late or extend the song service past our allotted time, we have infringed upon someone else's ministry time. This may possibly prevent them from having adequate time to accomplish their goals. Many times, some part of the service has to be cut out completely so that the service can get back on its original schedule. This means that someone's work will have to be altered or forfeited. If your tardiness or lack of adherence to your allotted time causes someone not to be able to present what they have prepared, then you have shown a great disrespect to that individual.

In our book ***Lifting Him Up***, co-authored with my former pastor, Dr. Dick Bernal, he listed ten things that pastors dislike about worship leaders. The first thing he mentioned that bothers pastors is when worship consistently does not start on time. The second thing was not stopping on time. If the pastor has to cut his sermon short or feel like he has to rush because you took too much time, you just might be in trouble. It is imperative that you use whatever authority you have to start the service on time so that you can finish on time. Your job is to adequately accomplish all that you planned to do according to God's mandate in the amount of time given by the senior pastor.

Establish and maintain order

When I first started as worship leader at Jubilee Christian Center, the congregation would mill around talking and visiting prior to the beginning of the song service. They were undisciplined and casual about finding a seat before the service. I would start the music and many of them would continue to laugh and talk as if the music was not really an important part of the service.

That type of attitude would always annoy me and grieve my heart. I considered their behavior as rude to the leader and an insult to God. After all, entering into praise and worship is both an invitation for God to manifest His presence and the acknowledgment of His presence in the midst of His people.

It is a grievous insult to ignore the Lord in His own house. I took this concern to Pastor Dick. I didn't know many of the people in the church at that time, and I did not know how he felt about this issue. I thought maybe these people were his friends or important people within the church membership. I found out that several of these people were his friends and big givers in the church.

Know your limitations

My esteem and admiration for Pastor Dick skyrocketed when he told me to do what I needed to do to bring these people to order. He gave me the authority to establish and create the proper environment for the presence of the Lord. With the assurance of the pastor's support, I began calling the disruptive people by name, and telling them over the microphone to stop talking and find a seat. If I didn't know them by name, I would send the ushers over to those disruptive people to bring them to order.

After the embarrassment of hearing their names called over the microphone or being escorted to their seats, they learned to curb their frivolity and respect the order of the worship service.

Use your authority wisely

Those who have been given authority must exercise it with boldness, but temper it with love. I'm not saying that you must be a tyrant, but you must use your authority and control the environment. Jesus, the King, is in your midst and the appropriate behavior must be demonstrated. The King must be honored and respected. Remember that He is the guest of honor and we are His subjects in His house. We are the invited ones.

People don't want to follow anyone who is timid and afraid. No one wants to follow someone who is uncertain about where they are going. People are looking for someone to lead them with confidence and boldness. The church needs someone who demonstrates that they know where they are going, how to get there, and what's going to happen when they arrive. These actions brings security and confidence.

It is easy to follow this type of person because we all have a tendency to trust them. They have a message and a mission which they have embraced in their hearts. It is with zeal and confidence that they determine to achieve their goals. God instructed Joshua to be bold and courageous. Young Joshua was instructed in the

Bible,"Be strong and of good courage, for to this people you shall divide as an inheritance the land which I swore to their fathers to give them" (Joshua 1:6, NKJV).

Joshua had to be bold and courageous because a military campaign had to be waged against the giants in the land. To some, the Israelites looked liked grasshoppers in comparison to the inhabitants of the land.

Fear had been the cause of their parents dying in the wilderness. They refused to face the obstacles before them even though God had promised them the victory and the land. God had performed miracles for them many times in Egypt and in the wilderness, but they still refused to go in and take what God had promised to give them.

Caleb and Joshua were not afraid at all. With authority and confidence, they went in and took the promised land without fear or intimidation. When God is with you, He is bigger than the world against you.

Demonstrate love and respect

You need to boldly let the people know that you love them. Tell them that you love them. Don't be afraid to show kindness and grace as you lead them.

The congregation will sing more confidently when the song key is in a comfortable range.When you teach new songs, make sure that they are written in a key that is reasonably comfortable for all the people to sing. Sometimes it is important for leaders to change the key of a recorded song so that the local congregation can sing it without a great degree of difficulty.

You need to sing in your range. If a song is too high or too low and you are unable to change the key of the song, consider having one of the other singers on the worship team sing lead on that particular song.

Make eye contact with the people

Don't be afraid to look at the people when you lead them. The worship leader needs to know that the people are following him. They need to see your eyes. Personally, I don't trust anyone who can't look straight into my eyes when they address me.

Smile and demonstrate the joy of the Lord. A simple smile will tear down the invisible barrier that exists between people. In most cases when you smile at someone, they will smile back. When that barrier comes down, people are more willing to lose some of their shyness and inhibitions. A smile goes a long way. Thich Nhat Hanh, a Vietnamese Monk and writer said, "Sometimes your joy is the source of your smile, but sometimes your smile can be the source of your joy." A smile is the first expression of joy. Let there be joy in the house of the Lord!

Encourage the people to greet and show love to one another. It was said by Mother Teresa of Calcutta, "Every time you smile at someone, it is an action of love, a gift to that person, a beautiful thing." The love of God will bind us together in unity and harmony.

Be sensitive to your congregation

Hymns are boring to most young people. Rock, rap and hip-hop have too much energy for most senior citizens. However, they both have their place in the body of Christ. Choose songs that are relevant to the age group to which you are ministering. The apostle Paul encourages us in Colossians 3:16, "sing psalms, hymns and sacred songs" (TEV). By presenting a variety of genres of music, you will be sure to touch each generation represented in your congregation.

Avoid tongue lashing

Choose to speak those things which edify and minister grace to the hearers. Don't yell at people if you don't get your desired response. Sometimes the people will not sing with the passion with which you want them to sing. Sometimes it seems as if they really don't want to praise God at all. There may be times when it doesn't seem as if the people care if the presence of God shows up or not.

These are the times when your flesh wants to tongue lash each one of them individually, and remind them of how good God has been to them.

You want to rebuke each one of them personally on behalf of the Lord. However, it is better to lead them where you want them to go, rather than drive them there.

Notice what Jesus said in John 10:2-4:

> *But he who enters by the door is the shepherd of the sheep. To him the door-keeper opens, and the sheep hear his voice; and he calls his own sheep by name and leads them out. And when he brings out his own sheep, he goes before them; and the sheep follow him, for they know his voice* (NKJV).

In these verses, we learn that the good shepherd **leads** the sheep. He does not have to drive or harass them to get to the right place. Because he has developed a relationship of trust and love, the sheep will faithfully follow his vocal command.

Teach the people whenever possible

Take every opportunity that you have to teach the congregation how to behave in the presence of our King. Use scriptural references to reinforce your goals when you teach. Scripture clearly shows us that there is a time to sing, to kneel, to bow, to clap, to stand, to shout and to lift our hands. As a worship leader, it is your responsibility to make sure that the people honor the King in a proper and responsible manner.

The Effective *P&W* Leader Must:

- Learn the language of music
- Take private lessons, if necessary
- Memorize the music

SEVEN

KEY #6: SKILL

Learn the language of music

Every professional field has its own language. Firemen and law enforcement officers have their language. Doctors and lawyers have their own language and professional terminology. Even Christians have buzz words that are used only in Christian circles. Very few people outside of Christianity use words like *anointing, atonement* and *propitiation.*

Musicians have terminology that is unique to the music profession. Many church musicians and singers are self-taught and may not know how to properly communicate with others in this arena. I think it is imperative that anyone who wants to remain in music for any length of time must at least learn the basic terms, and have a fundamental understanding of music. If you expect others in the music field to respect and appreciate you, you must be able to speak and communicate properly.

Take private lessons, if necessary

If you are a self-taught singer or musician, you should take the time to get private lessons or enroll in a local school that will help you gain understanding of your craft. Proverbs 13:16 says that good understanding wins favor. Talent will attract admiration, knowledge will gain respect, wisdom and understanding will open the door to favor.

Memorize the music

Learn the words to the songs. If people are going to honor you by giving you a platform to present your gifts and talents, I feel that you should honor those people by properly preparing yourself. When you commit a song to memory it is much easier to deliver the song with confidence and poise as you stand before the people. Of course, there are certain occasions when you are asked to sing a special song and you haven't been given the proper amount of time to learn the song (weddings, funerals, pastoral requests, etc.). If this happens, go ahead and use the sheet music as a reference. But if you are singing the song on a regular basis, you should learn it.

Musicians, try to learn the music by heart. Just as I encourage singers to commit songs to memory, I also challenge musicians and background vocalists to do the same. It only takes a few passes through a song to memorize it. Most of the praise and worship choruses that we sing in our churches today are musically simple and have few, but very important, words.

If I had to watch an actor read his script in a serious dramatic presentation, I would be very disappointed with the performance regardless of how good the script. When songs or scripts are read from a text it gives the listener or viewer a feeling that the message is coming from a third party. On the other hand, when the listener can see the eyes and the expressions of the presenter, the audience or congregation feels a sense of intimacy and identification with the them.

The Effective *P&W* Leader Must:

- Be sensitive to God and the people
- Sing songs in keys that are within everyone's range
- Provide arrangements that everyone can follow
- Choose congregational songs
- Choose the right genre for the congregation
- Match the volume with the mood
- Choose the right song for the right moment
- Eliminate solos during congregational worship
- Know when to release the people to pray and sing in the spirit

EIGHT

KEY #7: SENSITIVITY

Be sensitive to God and the people

Praise and worship leaders, you must remember that your position is not to be used as a stepping-stone for a recording contract. It is not your show. Your goal is to usher the people of God into His presence. Leading praise and worship is more than just leading people in singing. You must create an environment for God to manifest His holy presence. You must be sensitive first to the Holy Spirit, second to your pastor and third to your congregation.

Always remember that the majority of the people in the congregation are not as skilled as the worship leader. They haven't developed their vocal range, and their musical skills are relatively limited compared to yours. Your responsibility is to lead the people, but you must be careful, sensitive and observant so that you do not present music that the people cannot follow.

Sing songs in keys that are within everyone's range

Songs should be chosen in keys which everyone can sing. High tenors and high sopranos who are worship leaders may have to change some songs to a lower key so that the mass of the people can sing the song in a comfortable range. You may also arrange for another singer to lead the song in a different key. The most important thing is that the people are not straining to follow the person who is leading the song. When people struggle to sing a song, they are distracted from true worship. They cannot worship in pain and discomfort. The wrong key will definitely be a distraction or hindrance to worship, and you never want that to be the case. The music should enhance the entire experience.

Provide arrangements that everyone can follow

Make sure that the song arrangements are simple and easy so that even the most musically challenged people in the congregation can at least follow along, participating with their joyful noises. God appreciates a joyful noise. Psalms 66:1 says, "Make a joyful noise unto God, all ye lands." Always remember that the goal of the worship leader is to engage all of the people in praise and worship unto our Lord.

Choose congregational songs

Praise and worship is not a spectator event. All of the people should be involved or engaged. Even the people who can't sing should be encouraged and invited to make a joyful noise. Some songs are more soloist songs that are to be presented as a tribute to the Lord. The songs for praise and worship should allow the entire congregation to participate. Don't just choose your pet songs or songs that make you look good. Choose your songs prayerfully.

Choose the right genre for the congregation

If you are trying to lead youth, you will not win favor and confidence as their leader with hymns that were written over 100 years ago. You must provide songs with words, rhythms and melodies that are consistent with their age group. If you are leading a group of inner city African-Americans, you will not win them over with a country and western style of music. When leading senior citizens, make sure the song list includes songs that are near and dear to their heart. You don't want to alienate people from God's presence by your song choices. Choose songs that will help people enter in to God's presence.

Match the volume with the mood

Songs that are sweet and intimate need to be presented with less volume than songs which are high-energy and aggressive in nature. A high-energy song like "Celebrate Jesus" requires volume to be effective. Quiteness is a contradiction to the word "celebration." Celebrations are meant to be loud, exciting and jovial. They should be performed at full voice with hands clapping, feet dancing, instruments wailing, shouts and joyful expressions.

On the other hand, a sweet song like "Change My Heart, Oh God" should be passionate, intimate and sincere. It should be sung as if the singer is face to face with God. Intimacy is the key. When my wife and I want to be intimate, we draw close to each other and speak softly with direct eye-to-eye contact and hold each other close. We don't hold each other close and shout in the other's face.

The event determines the type of expression that should be used. I heard Tommy Tenny once say, "When my wife is in the car backing out of the driveway and I am standing in the doorway sending her off, I will yell, 'I love you!' But when she returns home and I lovingly embrace her in my arms, I will whisper sweetly to her, 'I love you, darling.'"

Many of the songs that we sing during a praise and worship service will dictate the type of expressions that should be demonstrated by the people. When the song lyrics speak of lifting hands, the appropriate response would be the lifting of hands. Should the song be about shouting and dancing, then the leader should encourage the congregation to dance and shout. If the song makes reference to kneeling before the Lord, then kneeling is the appropriate gesture for the people. As I mentioned earlier, don't harrass the congregation; be the leader and model of the appropriate behavior during worship.

Choose the right song for the right moment

Making your song list is one of the most important parts of the praise and worship service. Your song choice should cause the intensity to increase as the service progresses. If the wrong song is sung, it can change the entire tone for the worse. An experienced worship leader will know by the Holy Spirit if the wrong song is about to be presented. Even if the next song on the song list is your favorite song, you must yield to what the Lord is saying by His Spirit. When the right changes are made, you are more apt to experience the manifested presence of God. That's why it is so important to continually pray and be sensitive to what the Holy Spirit is saying as the service progresses. More than anything, God wants to be a part of the service, but He must have the right environment for His Holy presence. Some song choices are as inappropriate as a blues song being sung at a birthday party.

Eliminate solos during congregational worship

Generally solos or showcase type songs will not allow the whole congregation to engage in singing during the service. It is easy for the service to turn into a concert setting. You do not want it to become a spectator event. Your goal is to engage as many people as possible. You want all of the people to physically enter into the praise and worship experience. Unity helps to usher in the manifested presence of God. It is an example of togetherness before the Lord when the people join together singing the same song. A great example of the power of unity can be found in 2 Chronicles 5. When the singers, musicians and priests began to minister together in one accord the presence of the Lord filled the temple in such an awesome way that they had to fall down on their faces before the Lord. On many occasions, I have experienced the presence of God in this way during a service.

Know when to sing in the Spirit

The Bible instructs us on how to sing whether alone or in a congregation. 1 Corinthians 14:15 says, "I will sing with the spirit, and I will sing with the understanding also." There is a time and a place to sing from the things we know and there is a time to allow our spirits to sing unto God.

As you spend time in His presence privately, you will become finely tuned to His leading. In congregational worship, singing in the spirit will become an extension of your worship experience. As you sense the crescendo of God inhabiting the worship, you can release the congregation to enter.

If you have not experienced this intimacy in your private worship, you will probably not recognize the opportunity when it presents itself during corporate worship.

As the worship leader, you will need to be sensitive to the pastor as to whether this expression is appropriate congregational worship.

The Effective *P&W* Leader Must:

- Give guidelines and rules
- Honor the God of order
- Prepare an operations manual

NINE

KEY #8: ORGANIZATION

Give guidelines and rules

Everyone in the music department needs to have a clear understanding of the rules and policies.

Written guidelines will help people know and understand what is expected of them. The answers to most problems and issues can be resolved simply by developing a set of mandates to which your group can quickly refer.

When you don't have any written outlines for behavior, people will throw off restraint and make their own rules. The activities and attitudes that are born out of chaos can cause misunderstanding and confusion.

People need guidelines and rules. Imagine what it would be like if there were no written laws for highways or neighborhood streets. Everyone would do what they felt was right in their own eyes. People would lose consideration for others and assume that their way was the only correct way.

Remember the problems faced by Moses in the wilderness after he had delivered the people from the bondage in Egypt? The people had no laws or guidelines. When Moses went to the mountain-top to meet with God, the people made their own god and began to worship it. When there is no law, you will have lawlessness. Rebellion, revolt, uprising, upheaval, revolution and mutiny will occur when there are no laws.

Honor the God of order

God likes things to be done decently and in order. The devil is the author of confusion. Philosopher John Locke said, "Where there is no law there is no freedom." The Bible says in 2 Corinthians 3:17, "Now the Lord is that Spirit: and where the Spirit of the Lord is, there is liberty." Enforcing rules and policies to gain order will bring greater freedom to enter into worship, and usher in God's presence.

Without laws or rules you have no basis for disciplinary action.

People will engage in all types of inappropriate behavior when no boundaries are established. You must establish what is right and wrong behavior through a set rules and policies. Rules serve as a guideline for acceptable behavior and specifies the consequences for violating them. Studies show that children find security when they have rules and boundaries. We want to provide security and safety in our department where people can have a reasonable expectation for what they will encounter.

Prepare an operations manual

To those who ask me about developing a music department, I always recommend they start by creating an operations manual which outlines the specific ordnances that their department embraces. Make sure that all of the members receive a copy of the manual. Be sure to give a copy to new members as soon as you accept them into the music department. It is a good idea to take some rehearsal time a couple of times a year to review the manual and allow people to ask questions. Everyone needs to have a clear understanding of what is expected of them.

Make sure that the pastor gives his approval of your operations manual before you pass it out to the members. Give him a copy for his files, and if he has suggestions or corrections make those changes immediately.

As a leader, you must insist on appropriate conduct from all of the members of your group. Never place friendship above your responsibility as a leader. If it works out that you can be a friend, that is good; however, remember that as a leader of God's people, you are responsible to God and your church leaders. Don't let friendship cloud your judgment or cause you to have favoritism among the members.Your operations manual should include some of the following items:

1. *Service schedule, place and times*
   Each individual service of the week needs to be listed, along with the time and location of that service. Also, include the time to report prior to each service.

2. *Rehearsal schedule, place and times*
   Each individual rehearsal of the week should be listed, along with the time and place of that rehearsal.

3. *Dress code*
   When I travel, I speak with my team about what is appropriate to wear. Some churches are offended by women in slacks or sleeveless shirts. My main underlying dress code is to wear things that are modest and decent.
   a. Everyone in the department should

be aware of the service dress code (robes, suit and tie, dress or pants etc.).

b. The dress code should also inform each member of apparel that may be forbidden (cutoffs, shorts, jeans, T-shirts, flip-flops, halter tops, etc.).

4. *Disciplinary actions*
   a. Illegal, immoral, and non-Christian behavior must always be dealt with swiftly and firmly, according to clearly defined directives in your operations manual.
   b. All disciplinary actions must coincide with the denomination, the local church and the local civil laws and ordinances.
   c. Department leaders must know their limitations in regard to counseling, suspensions and dismissals.

5. *Church chain of command*
   Everyone must submit and respect the authority of those over the church and the anointed representatives of the church.

   - Pastor and spouse
   - Associate pastors
   - Elders and deacons

6. *Department chain of command*
   Everyone must submit to and respect the authority of those over the music department and its' appointed representatives.

   - Music pastor/director
   - Worship leader
   - Chief musician
   - Choir director
   - Section leaders

7. *Dues*
   If applicable. Some do; some don't.

8. *Appropriate or inappropriate behavior*
   Chewing gum, candy, water, mints, etc.

9. *Fines*
   Different from dues; fines are the results of a disciplinary action.

10. *Seasonal productions*
    Christmas, Easter, Harvest and Holiday productions need special instructions. They often involve people who are outside of the regular music department.

11. *Outreaches*
    Outreaches often take people away from the church campus. These off campus events need special instruc-

tions. They are usually held on public property or in private institutions where the public is invited. The dos and don'ts need to be clearly outlined.

12. *Retreats/Advances*
    These outings allow the music department to get away to a secluded place to pray, seek the Lord and bond with each other. Once again, the dos and don'ts need to be established, especially in the area of bonding. Remember to keep the retreat a spiritual and holy experience.

13. *Conferences and seminars*
    These are special opportunities for groups or individuals to meet and exchange thoughts and ideas with members of other churches and Christian ministers having like skills, talents and values. The delegates who go to these events are ambassadors of your congregation. They need to know and understand what is expected of them and how they must behave. Their behavior will be a direct reflection of the level of teaching and discipline being practiced in your church and music department.

14. *Missions opportunities*
    Missionary work can be short-term or

long-term. Quite often, money has to be raised for these trips, or the church may pay for it out of a designated fund. There must be clear instructions about who is qualified to go on these trips and their goals.

Guidelines must be established in regard to integrity, spending, morality, spirituality and amiability. Your ambassador to the mission field is not only representing the kingdom of heaven, but they are also the face of your congregation to a foreign people.

An example of this type of outreach can be seen in my own ministry. When I travel with a band, I make sure they know what is expected of them. They represent the Lord Jesus and my ministry while on trips. If we are meeting royalty, I expect my team to know how to bow or curtsy. They must know when to say, "Your Highness" or "Her Royal Majesty." The people who travel with me understand that they are expected to eat what is served when we are the guests of honor. Some cultures honor you with a special food that we might not normally eat in our culture. Anytime you reject their offering of honor, you risk being an offense to them.

Develop an operations manual, and take it to your pastor for approval. Once it has his support, copy and hand it out to the music department. Take time to go over it with the group. If you do not live by the manual, the group will not live by it either. If you respect the manual, your department will respect it, also.

The Effective *P&W* Leader Must Know:

- What is a choir?
- Choirs can be formal or informal
- History of scriptural choirs
- History of sanctuary choirs

TEN

The Importance of a Choir

What is a choir?

A choir is merely a group of singers singing together. They can be a mixture of men and women, all men, all women, adults and children, or all children. There are also many all boy or all girl choirs.

Choirs can be formal or informal

Formal choirs are separated into sections based on the range and timber of the voices. Most formal choirs will be sectioned into three or four groups: SAT (Soprano, Alto, Tenor) or SATB (soprano, alto, tenor, bass). Generally, formal choirs will require an audition so that each voice can be placed in the proper section according vocal range and voice timber.

Each section will have its own set of notes or parts to sing. When these parts are simultaneously executed they are capable of producing beautiful music for those who listen.

Informal choirs are generally people who come together simply for the joy of singing. They may not have any formal training nor any concept of harmony, blend or music theory. They are not auditioned and are allowed to sing any part they want to sing. Because of the lack of discipline toward the harmony parts of a song, most of the singers will sing the melodies as best they can. They will not sound as good as a formal choir, but they will generally make a joyful noise.

Choirs can be great in numbers or small. Groups of less than 10 people are often referred to as a *choral ensembles*. In church circles, they may also be called *worship teams* or *back line singers*. I have personally participated in choirs that contain thousands of singers and have also sung in choirs that consisted of less than ten people.

History of scriptural choirs

One of the earliest references to a choir in the Bible is found in the book of Exodus. After the children of Israel had crossed the Red Sea, Moses wrote a song describing the deliverance of God's people and the destruction of the Egyptian army.

Then sang Moses and the children of Israel this song unto the LORD, and spake, saying, I will sing unto the LORD, for he hath triumphed gloriously: the horse and his rider hath he thrown into the sea (Exodus 15:1).

And Miriam the prophetess, the sister of Aaron, took a timbrel in her hand; and all the women went out after her with timbrels and with dance. And Miriam answered them, Sing ye to the LORD, for he hath triumphed gloriously; the horse and his rider hath he thrown into the sea (Exodus 15:20,21).

The children of Israel had been captives in Egypt for over 400 years. They had been subjected to harsh slavery and persecution. Because of their enslavement, it is possible that this generation of Hebrews did not know how to read or write. Even though the events of their deliverance would be chronicled by Moses, the people would not have been able to read about them.

These references in Exodus are a song that Moses wrote and called upon the people to sing. It would be one of the ways that all the children of Israel would remember the mighty acts that God had performed on their behalf. They would sing this song over and over to themselves and to their children, reminding the people that Jehovah is the one true God and the one who delivered them from the harsh enslavement of the Egyptians.

Each time they sang that song of praise and victory they celebrated the power and ability of their heavenly Lord. Miriam and the Hebrew women led the singing as they danced throughout the camp with tambourines.

This, of course, would have been an informal choir. It appears that there was no audition for singers. All of the women seemingly were invited to participate in the singing and dancing.

In this passage of Scripture, we are able to see how valuable and important a choir can be to the people of God. When the congregation comes together it is important to review what God has done for us. Church choirs musically recite testimonies, praises, adorations and divine interventions that God has made on our behalf. They sing songs that reflect the goodness and the matchless love of God for His people. The songs tell about His faithfulness to those who call upon His name. One such song is found in 1 Samuel 29:5 which records, "Is not this David, of whom they sang one to another in dances, saying, Saul slew his thousands, and David his ten thousands?"

Choirs are not limited to choir lofts and sanctuaries. In the verse above, the women came together and sang about the great triumphs of David. They danced and sang with joy and excitement, celebrating the feats of David compared to the victories of their ruling king, Saul. The streets were filled with melodies and lyrics about the new champion in the ranks of the Hebrew military.

The following Scriptures depict more scriptural references to choirs or groups of singers singing together.

> *And they ministered before the dwelling place of the tabernacle of the congregation with singing, until Solomon had built the house of the LORD in Jerusalem: and [then] they waited on their office according to their order (1 Chronicles 6:32).*

Here we see the choir ministering before the Lord. This choir was a formal choir made up of Levites who had been ordained by King David. They were chosen because of their excellence in music and singing. They ministered continually in the tabernacle at Mount Zion, offering the sacrifice of praise up to God.

Each singer had an assignment and a time for their musical service before the Lord.

> *And David and all Israel played before God with all [their] might, and with singing, and with harps, and with psalteries, and with timbrels, and with cymbals, and with trumpets (1 Chronicles 13:8).*

In King David's first attempt to bring the ark of the covenant from Kirjathjearim to Mount Zion, we see that the choir was accompanied by musicians. This was probably an informal group of singers since all of Israel was invited to join in the singing.

> *Also Jehoiada appointed the offices of the house of the LORD by the hand of the priests the Levites, whom David had distributed in the house of the LORD, to offer the burnt offerings of the LORD, as [it is] written in the law of Moses, with rejoicing and with singing, [as it was ordained] by David (2 Chronicles 23:18).*

This choir was a formal choir. It was a choir for whom King Jehoiada took full responsibility. He selected the singers and musicians who would minister in the house of the Lord. They were chosen because of their excellence and skill.

> *And the children of Israel that were present at Jerusalem kept the feast of unleavened bread seven days with great gladness: and the Levites and the priests praised the LORD day by day, [singing] with loud instruments unto the LORD (2 Chronicles 30:12).*

Choirs ministered at the appointed feasts. We see here that the feast would last for seven days and the singing was a major part of the festival celebrations.

> *And Jeremiah lamented for Josiah: and all the singing men and the singing women spake of Josiah in their lamentations to this day, and made them an ordinance in Israel: and, behold, they [are] written in the lamentations (2 Chronicles 35:25).*

At the death of King Josiah, the men's choir and the women's choir lamented for their beloved King. Since women had lesser social status than men, it is unlikely that the two choirs sang together. Nevertheless, we see that both choirs were ordained to minister in music.

> *Beside their manservants and their maidservants, of whom [there were] seven thousand three hundred thirty and seven: and they had two hundred forty and five singing men and singing women (Nehemiah 7:67).*

The people of Judah were allowed to return to Jerusalem from Babylon with the prophet Ezra. At that time, they were careful to bring with them two hundred singers, both men and women.

Apparently it was important to the Jewish people to have a dedicated choir of men and women to re-establish a high standard of worship in Jerusalem.

> *And at the dedication of the wall of Jerusalem they sought the Levites out of all their places, to bring them to Jerusalem, to keep the dedication with gladness, both with thanksgivings, and with singing, [with] cymbals, psalteries, and with harps (Nehemiah 12:27).*

When the walls of Jerusalem were rebuilt and dedicated the celebration included singers and musicians committed to honoring the Lord.

There are many other Scriptures related to choirs and group singing. These are just a few.

History of the sanctuary choir

Medieval Music

In the 4th century, a style of choir singing called the *Gregorian chant* was used in the Catholic churches in Italy. This style of music was primarily sung a cappella (without musical instruments) by the monks of the church. The Gregorian chants are still being used in many traditional services in the Catholic Church.

The Gregorian chant was named after Pope Gregory 1. Many pictures of him depict the Holy Spirit, in the form of a dove, on his shoulder singing the melodies that would be presented to the monks. The monks would take these Gregorian chants and use them in their times of ministry.

This music was generally sung in unison; however, there are times when polyphony would be sang by soloists. The soloists would sing two distinctly different parts.

Renaissance Music

The 15th century introduced a new style of choral music called renaissance music. Choral music had become very popular throughout all

Europe, and many writers were writing formal music for the Catholic Church masses.

Renaissance music introduced advanced levels of music theory, composition and performance. Medieval music was primarily limited to one melody and occasionally had a counter melody. Having a third melody had previously been considered *dissonant*. With the addition of the third melody, more range was added to the composition; thus demanding more vocal skill, vocal range and more accuracy of pitch. This music created a demand for smoothness and blend from the voices.

Many musical instruments were born during the Renaissance period. Instruments that were used in secular music were now being used by the church. Each instrument had its own style and purpose. The instruments most commonly used were horns, strings, percussions and woodwinds.

Secular music produced small choral groups called *madrigals*. These groups generally sang songs about love, drinking and eating. The madrigals generally stirred up the spirit in the parties and the pubs in Western Europe.

Baroque Music

Baroque music began in the early 17th century. This period introduced more elaborate and difficult works of music. Music theory and imitative counterpoint developed greatly during this era. The baroque era challenged writers to expand the size, range and complexity of their compositions. It was during this time that the opera came into being.

The main strength of Baroque music was its unity of emotion, ornamentation, variation in rhythm and improvisation.

It was during the Baroque period that George Frideric Handel wrote *Messiah*. This is one of the most popular and celebrated choral works in western music. The "Hallelujah Chorus" is a part of Handel's *Messiah*.

At certain times of the year in America, many choirs will join together in civic auditoriums just to sing this work of art together. It is truly a masterpiece.

The Importance

The more understanding that a praise and worship director has about the history of choirs, the better able to utilize the strengths of choirs and avoid the weaknesses.

Friend, be confident in God's calling on your life. Not doing so gives the enemy an open door to bring you down. If the enemy can get you to doubt your identity in Christ and in God's ability to do with you what He purposes to do, then the enemy has won.

The Effective *P&W* Leader Must Know:

- The role of a contemporary choir
- Who should be in a church choir
- How to select choir members
- Qualifications of a choir director
- Issues in governing a choir
- Law -vs- policy
- The choir specifics to include in the operations manual
- The time for disciplinary action

ELEVEN

The Contemporary Church Choir

The role of a contemporary choir

We have already acknowledged the importance and value placed on choirs and singing groups in the Bible. They help us to remember the things which God has done for us. Through their music, they remind us of the acts, works, deeds, promises, character and attributes of our Almighty Creator. They lead us in songs and expressions of worship to our Heavenly Father. These songs of worship help us to tell God how much we love and honor Him.

Choirs and worship teams (small choirs) encourage and inspire congregations to sing with them and magnify the Lord together. Of course, these will sing the harmony parts and enhance the beauty of the music. However, worship and praise should never be a spectator event. King David wrote in Psalm 34:3 "magnify the Lord with me and let us exalt His name together."

Too often people in the congregation say they can't sing and would prefer to let the singers on the platform do all of the singing. God, however, requires everyone to make an effort to praise Him. There is no such thing as silent praise and worship. The Scriptures command praise and worship from every one who is alive and breathing.

In Psalms 150:6 King David commanded, "Let everything that has breath praise the Lord." When a king commands something it is not to be thought of as a good idea, a suggestion or something to consider; it immediately becomes law.

Choirs also provide special musical presentations to bless and edify the body of Christ.

Who should be in a church choir?

A church choir should consist of members who:

- Have a genuine love for singing and a passion for choral music.
- Have a willingness to take the time to learn the music, both individually and with the rest of the group.
- Are able to cooperate and mix congenially with other singers.

- Can sing on pitch and have a good sense of rhythm. This is very important because the beauty of the music is always determined by the accuracy of pitch and the preciseness of timing.
- Are willing to make a time commitment. Participation in a choir will require weekly scheduled rehearsals (sometimes more frequently for special events) and designated times for services and performances.
- Submit to the leadership of the group. Each member must recognize and submit to the leadership of the director. The director will constantly give directives and assignments; each member is expected to comply with these mandates.
- Live a lifestyle consistent with the Bible and the doctrines of their church. Choir members should be Christians growing in the knowledge of the Word of God and living according to the doctrines of the church. They may not be considered church leaders, but they are ambassadors of their church to their individual communities, family members and neighbors.

How to select choir members

Open invitation

Many choir directors, especially choirs from small churches, are excited to have anyone who likes music participate in the choir. They offer an open invitation and receive everyone to provide an opportunity to sing from the choir loft. They may or may not have musical knowledge or basic skills. Of course, you can always tell when there are untrained and uneducated vocalists in a choir. The group may be exciting, but the quality of the sound will be lacking.

Audition

When choir members are auditioned, each individual singer is chosen according to his or her skill level, timber of voice, pitch placement and sometimes their ability to read music. The musical sounds of an auditioned choir will always be cleaner, more blended, more accurate in pitch and timing and more refined.

The auditioned choir will, in most cases, be able to perform a greater selection of songs and be able to learn the music much faster than a non-auditioned group.

Qualifications of a choir director

At the beginning of this book, we discussed the qualifications for a praise and worship leader. Many times the praise and worship leader may also be the person who leads the choir. However, in some churches, there will be a choir director who only ministers with and through the choir. The choir director may not be a soloist, but the praise and worship leader is always a soloist.

In the case where the choir director is different from the praise and worship leader, we find the following qualifications a must:

- Education - Anyone in leadership should know something about what they are trying to do. Continual education for leaders is essential.
- The choir director must have a basic understanding of music theory and harmony.
- One must have singing skills that enable them to demonstrate parts, intervals and rhythms correctly to the choir members.
- They must present themself before the choir with confidence, boldness, knowledge and purpose.
- They must be able to execute directing skills, hand signs and signals.
- The director must be able to work with musicians that accompany the choir.
- They must be able to place singers in the right sections according to their abilities.
- One must be able to rehearse individual sections.
- They must select music that the choir is capable of performing effectively.
- Directors must embrace leadership skills that motivate, inspire and challenge the

members of the choir, individually and collectively.

- Leadership abilities for the choir director should include the same requirements we stated for a worship leader. These qualifications have been addressed earlier in this book.
- Administrative abilities
- Mild pastoral training
- Vision is a necessity to go to the next level. A director should understand where they are and where they want to go and determine the route to get there.

Issues in governing a choir

- *Rules, policies and bylaws.* Every choir must have a code by which the group can effectively operate. When you don't have an established official code of order and conduct, the members will have a tendency to do whatever they want. When there is no single code to live by, you will have chaos, rebellion, disrespect and anarchy. People need to know their boundaries and limitations. When they have no laws, they will behave lawlessly and disorderly.

As I mentioned earlier, every group must have a written set of laws, policies, or rules clearly defined and easy to understand. This code of conduct must be presented to each member, old and new.

✦ *Punctuality.* Tardiness should be unacceptable and not tolerated in most situations. In my experience with groups of people, I have concluded that most of the excuses for tardiness are lies, half-truths, or the result of irresponsibility. I believe that there are some legitimate reasons for occasional tardiness; however, the person who plans well will allow time for emergencies and unexpected challenges which could slow them down.

I've picked up a saying along the way that goes like this:

To be early is commendable.
To be on time is expected.
To be late is unacceptable.

Tardiness cannot go unchecked in any member. When members see one person getting away with being late, others will use that as a license to be late, as well.

Compulsive tardiness can become habitual if it is not addressed. I once had a band member who loved the Lord with all of her heart. She was very talented and loved being part of the music department. I recognized her gift and anointing and tried to promote her as much as possible. Music was her passion. She had made a heart commitment to serve in every way possible.

However, she was late more times than not. Her excuse was always the same: she had to get her children ready. She had three children: six, four and two years old. With three small children needing constant attention, she needed an escape. Her participation in the music department was therapy for her. She was a true worshipper and I could see that God was going to use her in a wonderful way someday. Our music department was the weekly change of pace that helped her keep her personal life and her self-worth in proper prospective. Of course, she loved her husband and children, but playing in the band helped her maintain peace of mind in her very busy and hectic world.

Knowing that God's hand was on her life, I didn't want to dismiss her from the group for her constant tardiness, but I had to do something. In counseling with her, I realized that none of the other groups she had been in had ever questioned her about her tardiness because of her awesome gift. They were afraid that she might get offended and leave.

In our counseling sessions, I also learned that she had never learned any parenting skills. Many young men and women in our nation start families before they have any classes on how to be a parent. I asked one of the older mothers in our congregation to mentor her in parenting and family matters, and to give her tips on how she could be more efficient in taking care of her family. This would help her break the spirit of tardiness that had come over her.

She was happy to receive the counsel of the older lady. The young mother learned many clever ways in which she could save time, plan ahead, manage her home and combine certain activities.

I immediately, saw a difference in her. She overcame the tardiness and excelled to become not only one of the leaders in our music department, but went on to take important roles in other ministries of the church.

She had come to a place where fifteen to twenty minutes late was an acceptable habit, and I had to deal with it. I didn't want to lose her, but on the other hand, I was not going to accept that area of inappropriate behavior. She would not have changed if I had not confronted her.

Laws -vs- policy

Laws apply to all members of a group, from the most important to the least of all. When someone breaks a law, punishment or disciplinary action must be taken. No one is exempt from the laws that govern an organization. Laws cannot be changed or adjusted for any one person.

Unfortunately there is no grace woven into the letter of the law. Sometimes the laws that govern a group can seem harmful to people who are committed and faithful to the organization.

I personally prefer to govern with a set of policies instead of fixed laws. Policies can be changed or altered to address the uniqueness of a particular situation. Decisions and judgments may be made based on the character and history of the individual and his particular situation.

Years ago, while I was music pastor at Jubilee Christian Center, I had a memorable experience concerning laws versus policy. There were two horn players in our band and they were both excellent musicians. Each was dedicated to the church, God and the music department of the church. However, they were very different in character and personality.

I will identify them as Player A and Player B. Player A was a manager at the place of his employment. He was always prepared and ready for practice and the services. He always practiced his parts at home. When he came to the rehearsals, he helped other musicians execute and approach the music with the right attitude. Playing his horn was a serious part of his offering and a demonstration of his love to the Lord. He was a big help to me and our music director.

At the time, our church was having a serious growth spurt. We had five services per week: Wednesday night, Friday night, two on Sunday morning and one on Sunday night.

Player A was assigned to play on Friday nights and Sunday mornings. As the manager at his job, he would sometimes have a difficult time balancing his accounts and closing his store for the weekend. He would then have to get on the freeway and drive at a snail's pace in the traffic for nearly thirty miles. His job was very stressful and demanding. Playing his horn in the music department helped him bring his life to balance and order. He needed to be there on Friday nights.

Our policy was for everyone to meet in the band room thirty minutes before each service started. There were many times that player A would not get there thirty minutes before starting time. Because I knew his character, struggles and faithfulness, I would allow him to play anyway. I knew that he had done his best to get there as soon as he could and also how much he needed to play.

Because we governed ourselves with policies instead of laws, I could grant him grace and favor when those difficult times occurred. A strict law would have punished this man who had made the utmost effort to be there to render wholehearted service to the Lord.

Player B was a good horn player with a jovial spirit and personality. Everybody loved him and he kept all of us laughing with his jokes and antics. He had formerly played music in nightclubs and bars before giving his life to the Lord only a few years prior to coming to our church.

Player B, however, had a problem getting to practices and services on time; not because he had urgent responsibilities, he was just irresponsible. Unlike Player A, Player B had very few challenges when it came to getting to the church, but instead of coming into the church and preparing his horn, he would hang out in the parking lot talking to his friends (his personal fans).

After several episodes of being late with no good reason, I put him on suspension for three months after having a good counseling session with him. I was surprised at how well he accepted the correction and three month suspension.

During our counseling session, he revealed to me that no one had ever confronted him in such a bold way. He was such a good musician that other groups with whom he had played were afraid to confront him for fear he would be offended and leave them. I did not want to lose him, but I was not going to tolerate his blatant disrespect for our policies and procedures. If I had ignored his antics, it would have given license for others in the group to abuse our system of government.

I am happy to say that Player B did return after three months and submitted to the policies of our music department. He became one of our model members after a few years. To this day, he still thanks me for confronting him and causing him to analyze his character and future; it changed his life.

You might think that I practiced a double standard and I won't argue with you about that. I just know that different people need to be dealt with in different ways. God has blessed me with the ability to see the potential in people and try to help them reach the level of excellence that He has ordained for them. I could have penalized Player A for being late and suspended him for a time; but in doing that I would have denied him the opportunity to offer to God the gift which he so desperately needed to offer. A firm rule would have caused me to suspend him and possibly crush his spirit.

I don't use a democratic system of government for managing the organizations that I am placed over. God never ordained democracy. We are citizens of the kingdom of God. God refers us to the Holy Spirit and asks us to allow His Spirit to lead us into all truth and wisdom. "If any of you lacks wisdom, let him ask of God, who gives to all liberally and without reproach, and it will be given to him" (James 1:5).

The choir specifics to include in the operations manual

The music department's manul would address the overall guidelines for that department. In addition, the choir director would need to have specific rules outlined in the department's manual. It is imperative for all choir members to understand what is expected of them regarding attendance, rehearsals, behavior, dress, etc.

The time for disciplinary action

You must confront disrespect and rebellion head on; give no place for the enemy to come in and disrupt your efforts. We live in a world where people in every arena of life will challenge authority and leadership. At some time, you will be attacked by the enemy and your authority challenged. Your strength and commitment as a leader will be challenged. You must study your Bible and know the Word of God so you can fight your adversary with Scripture. "Study to show thyself approved unto God, a workman that needeth not to be ashamed, rightly dividing the word of truth" (2 Timothy 2:15). Every controversy should be met directly with Scripture. You cannot fight spiritual battles with your own opinion or the methods of the world. You must always know what God says about a matter; His way is the only way that He will honor.

There will be times when you have to execute disciplinary action. You must act with boldness, kindness and love. Sometimes wolves will show up in sheep's clothing. Have no patience with people who try to disrupt what God has called you to do. Harsh discipline will sometimes involve suspension or terminating someone from the music department. Always notify the pastor or elders over the department of what you are doing and why. Get their counsel and advice before dismissing someone. They should know the civil laws of your area or state, and how they may apply to any action that you are contemplating.

Pastors and elders will assist you in executing the necessary action. In my years as a music pastor, there were several people that I placed on suspension. Some of them received the correction and became better Christian workers, while others left the church. My pastor encouraged me and told me that if they could not accept correction, we did not want them as members of our congregation. On a few occasions, he cancelled a person's membership and applied for a court injunction that prohibited them from ever coming back to our church.

These cases are extreme and unusual; I hope you never have to deal with issues that call for such actions. If you set the standard high, your group will know that you mean business and intend to give God the best praise you can. God deserves the best we can give, and He is also expecting us to improve in our gifts and talents as we grow in our knowledge of Him.

I really hope that some of the ideas and testimonies of my experiences will help you in your quest to be the servant that God wants you to be. What I have shared has worked for me and has helped me to advance to new levels of service to our Lord. I am quite aware that there are many different expressions in the body of Christ. The things that have worked for me may not work for you. However, you are reading this book because you desire to go to the next level. This may be God's way of encouraging you; His way of equipping you to implement things that will cause your congregation to create an environment that allows God to manifest His presence in your services.

TWELVE

FINAL WORD

Thank you for allowing me to share my understanding and experiences with you. As I said, everything I have mentioned or written may not work for you in your arena of ministry or church exactly as it did in mine; however, they are definitely things to be considered in your quest for excellence as you labor in the kingdom of our Lord.

I have given you Scriptures and suggestions that I have applied to my own ministry issues. I found them to be the answers to resolving conflicts, building strong and lasting relationships, and most of all, creating the proper environment for God to manifest His holy presence during services and in my personal life.

God's Word will not return void. It will accomplish what He purposes for it to accomplish. He will perform His works through those who are willing to hear His voice and do what He calls them to do. It is true that God looks at our availability instead of our ability; however, He will put His ability with your ability and take you to the highest levels in ministry.

I challenge you to read His Word daily. Meditate on His Word continually. Pray without ceasing. In all things, give Him thanks. Let His praise continually be in your mouth.

This is my prayer for you:

Father, You have given me great understanding and wonderful experiences over the years. You have proven your Word is true and effective for those who trust and walk according to Your principles. As I have worshipped and praised You in spirit and truth, You have manifested Your presence over and over again in services and in my personal life.

Now Father, in the name of Jesus, Your Son, I speak blessings over those who read this book and apply the teaching to their own ministry according to their individual calling and responsibilities.

Lord, guide them and protect them. Magnify Yourself in them. Let Your glory be seen in them as they perform Your will and desires. Let Your desires be their desires. May they give You glory in all they do.

May they prosper in every arena of their lives. May their homes be blessed beyond measure, and may their health be strong and sufficient for every work that You anoint them to do.

In the name of Jesus. Amen.

Obedience to His will and His Word is the key to being an effective worship leader. He is looking for those who will worship in spirit and in truth. Go ahead and be the worshipper for whom God is looking.

Dr. Ron Kenoly and the RKM Worship Team would like to minister in your city. If you are interested in hosting an event with our team, please allow the following steps to guide you through the process.

- Fax or mail RKM an official letter of invitation on your ministry letterhead.
Fax: 407.226.2917
Mail: P. O. Box 2200, Windermere, FL 34786 USA

- The RKM Events Department will respond to your invitation by faxing you an Events Detail Questionnaire and Host's Responsibility Form. This will give you more information regarding the travel, lodging and financial goals of our Ministry Team.

- After these communications, your contact person and our Events Department will be able to work out details for a successful Ministry Event.

Email Events Coordinator at:
Events@RonKenoly.org.

Order Ron Kenoly Music & Books

www.RonKenoly.org

Powerful Hymns My Mother Sang

New hymn release serving as a tribute to Ron's mother containing the favorite classics: "His Eye is on the Sparrow," "How Great Thou Art," and "Holy, Holy, Holy."

Lift Him Up Collection

A great compilation of the best hits of Ron Kenoly. Includes "Beauty for Ashes" with Crystal Lewis.

Fill the Earth

Studio release by Ron Kenoly and High Praise. Includes "His Banner Over Us is Love" and "Smiling."

Solo Para Ti

A Spanish release filled with praise and worship to the Lord. Includes songs such as "Eres Mi Gozo," "Te Dedicamos Hoy" and "Recuerdame."

The Perfect Gift

A contemporary praisical, written by Ron Kenoly, celebrating the birth of Christ. Features the Kenoly Brothers and the Ron Kenoly Worship Team.

Dwell in the House

Ron Kenoly's first studio release includes "You Are" duet with Hillsong's Darlene Zschech.

We Offer Praises

Recorded in Fiuggi, Italy with a special appearance by the Kenoly Brothers. Includes "Joshua Generation" and "Mighty God."

Majesty

Recorded live at The Vines Center at Liberty University in Lynchburg, Virginia.

Welcome Home

Dove Award Winning Release.

High Places

Ron Kenoly's psalmist heart combines with his rich, soulful voice. Includes "Lift Him Up" and "God Is Able."

Sing Out With One Voice

Features a 350-voice choir, orchestra, dancers, banners, the African Children's Choir and much more. Includes:
"Oh, the Glory of Your Presence," "Sing Out" and "Ain't Gonna Let No Rock."

Lift Him Up

Includes: "Lift Him Up," "Ancient of Days" and "Let Everything That Has Breath."

God Is Able

Features the 120-voice Atlanta Praise and Worship Choir. Includes: "Use Me," "The Battle Is the Lord's" and "His Eye Is on the Sparrow."

Jesus Is Alive

Ron's first Hosanna! Music album, recorded live in San Jose, California. Includes: "Jesus Is Alive," "Making War in the Heavenlies" and "Hallowed Be Thy Name."

Parsons Publishing House
Tel: 850.867.3061
Info@ParsonsPublishingHouse.com
www.ParsonsPublishingHouse.com

ORDER ADDITIONAL COPIES

THE EFFECTIVE PRAISE & WORSHIP LEADER
by Dr. Ron Kenoly

What is a good worship leader? What does a pastor want in a worship leader? Use this book as a measuring stick for the anointed person you want to become. From his vast experience, Ron Kenoly shares insight into the office of the worship leader and offers eight keys for more effectiveness. Order today for only $10.95 + $3 S/H.

The PRIORITY OF PRAISE & WORSHIP
by Dr. Ron Kenoly

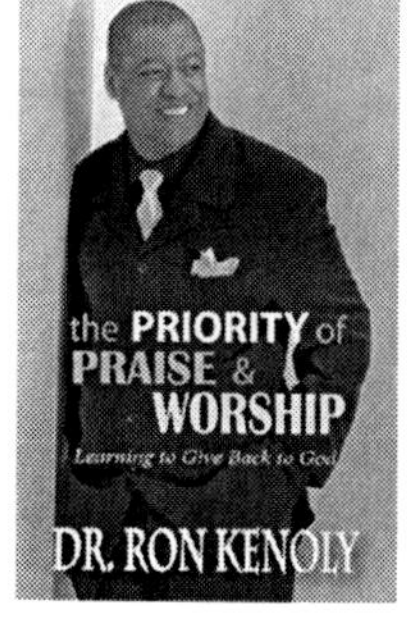

Ron Kenoly has stepped into a new season of ministry where his heart and vision is to mentor worshipers. Through this book, you will receive proven answers to issues from one of the nation's most anointed and experienced worship leading authorities. Each chapter is designed to take you to a higher level of excellence and effectiveness. Order your for only $12.95 + $3 S/H.

LIFTING HIM UP
by Ron Kenoly & Dick Bernal

Worship leader Ron Kenoly teams up with his pastor, Dick Bernal, in this practical guide to praise and worship. You'll learn how to enter into the Lord's presence, plus you'll gain insight into the scriptural role of praise and worship in your life and church. Order your copy today for only $12.95 + $3 S/H.

RELEASE YOUR WORDS IMPACT YOUR WORLD
by Darrell Parsons

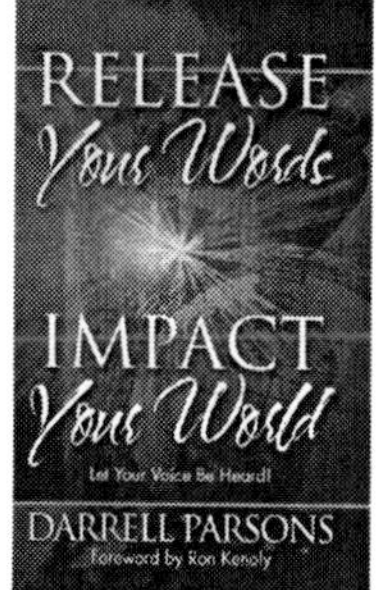

Your words can make a difference! God has done something in the life of every believer. He has placed treasures inside you that He wants to use to touch hearts and minds. The Lord wants to use you to touch your world! It's time to release your words to impact your world. The vision is for the appointed time and that time is now! Order your copy today for only $9.95 + $3 S/H.

PORTRAIT OF A PASTOR'S HEART
A Manual on Caring for the Sheep
by Bishop Gerald Doggett

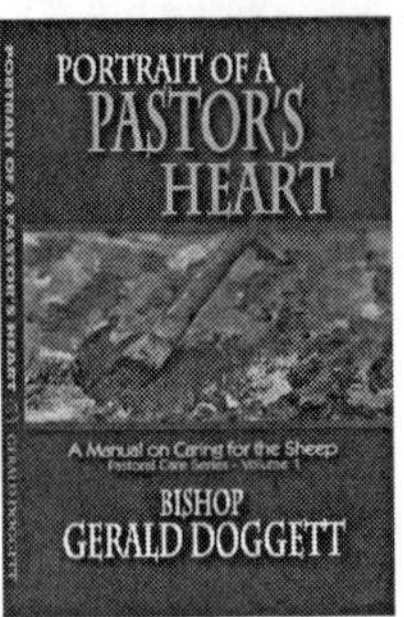

This book is a must for pastors, elders, students & laymen who want to learn how to care for the flock of God. Bishop Gerald Doggett paints a rare and intimate portrait of a pastor's heart after having served congregations for over thirty years. He covers TOPICS such as: Spirit of a Finisher, The Necessity of the Divine Call and A Beautiful Portrait of Preparation. Order your copy today for only $12.95 + $3 S/H.

MOUNTAIN VIEW - A Photo Collection
by Doris Beets

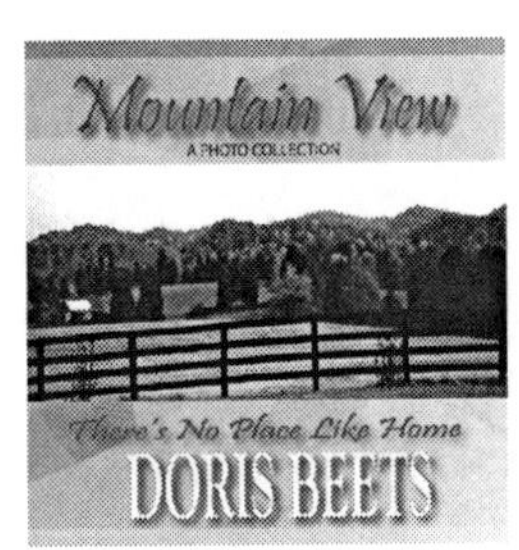

Contained in these pages is a pictorial discovery of a community where splendor is exemplified - where beauty is personified. Those who live here are enriched year after year by the beauty and bounty - by the grandeur and goodness - by the grace and glory of this beautiful land. In this book, Doris Beets attempts to give you a glimpse of the world that captured her heart over 75 years ago. Order your copy today for only $29.95 + $5 S/H.

WITH EVERY BEAT OF MY HEART
A Weekly Devotional
by Jeff North

Explore real life examples in real Christian living. ***Every Beat of My Heart*** takes the reader to a place where inspirational stories and poems stay upon their hearts and lips throughout the day. This book offers a practical message with a godly foundation to encourage, motivate and bring comfort (224 pages). Order today for only $14.95 + $4 S/H.

CAPTURING THE HEART OF GOD
Pleasing the Father in Everyday Life
by Diane Parsons

God created man for His good pleasure. Our most satisfying goal should be to bring delight to our Heavenly Father. Make it your goal today to do those things which please God. This book contains practical tips on capturing the heart of God and becoming His delight everyday. Order your copy for only $10.95 + $3 S/H.

LaVergne, TN USA
03 August 2010
191887LV00002B/10/P

9 781602 730045